# Creating Undetectable AI Generated Content©

Adam J. Lambert-Gorwyn

Imprint:
Independently Published

First Edition

Creating Undetectable AI Generated Content
Copyright © 2023 by Consultingly, LLC

Author:
Adam J. Lambert-Gorwyn

Cover & Interior Design:
Adam J. Lambert-Gorwyn

Typography:
Adam J. Lambert-Gorwyn

ISBN: 979-8-86608-987-1

Author's Note

"As we weave narratives with digital threads, let us remember that the true essence of content lies in its human touch."

**GPT-4**

# Table of Contents:

# Forward

Dear Content Marketers,

As the founder of Infinity Drafts, I am pleased to introduce you to this comprehensive guide on "Creating Undetectable AI-Generated Content." It's a culmination of our copywriting experience, and passion for redefining the way businesses create content in today's digital landscape.

In an era where content is king, the need for effective, engaging, and authentic copy has never been more crucial. AI provides us with tools to quickly generate powerful copy, but AI generated content has trouble being ranked by search engines. With the rise of AI detection systems, creating content that both resonates with human readers and evades the algorithms has become a formidable challenge.

This guide was born out of our desire of finding a solution to this challenge. Over the years, we've harnessed the capabilities of artificial intelligence, combined them with human creativity, and fine-tuned our approach to achieve a delicate balance between authenticity and AI.

Inside these chapters, you'll discover not only the intricacies of AI-generated copy but also the strategies, techniques, and ethics surrounding it. We've outlined the landscape of AI detection and offered insights into how to craft content using AI that remains undetectable. Additionally, we've shared real-world applications and success stories that demonstrate the impact of undetectable AI-generated copy.

I invite you to dig in, digest the information, and apply the ideas to your copywriting efforts. Remember that this is more than simply a guide; it's an invitation to embrace the future of AI content creation with confidence and creativity.

Thank you for joining us, and I look forward to a future where undetectable AI-generated copy becomes the norm, enabling businesses like yours to thrive in an ever-evolving digital world.

Happy Writing,

Adam J. Lambert-Gorwyn
Founder, Infinity Drafts

# Chapter 1: Introduction

## The Age of AI in Copywriting

In the rapidly evolving landscape of content creation, artificial intelligence (AI) has emerged as a powerful ally. Its transformative potential has touched every aspect of the digital realm, especially copywriting. AI has transitioned from a mere technological advancement to a cornerstone of modern content strategy.

This chapter embarks on an exploration of AI's evolution in copywriting, and why this transformation is pivotal in today's digital era. We will unravel the astonishing capabilities AI brings to the realm of written content, while also acknowledging the pressing concern—SEO risk—where search engines may detect and not include AI-generated text in search results.

## 1. AI's Evolution in Copywriting

Understanding AI's role in copywriting requires a grasp of its journey from infancy to maturity. Initially, AI-driven content creation was rudimentary, focusing on predefined patterns and templates. While these early endeavors were promising, they lacked the finesse to emulate the creativity and adaptability of human authors.

However, recent strides in AI, particularly in Natural Language Processing (NLP), have led to paradigm shifts in copywriting. Cutting-edge models, such as GPT (Generative Pre-trained Transformer), now showcase the ability to generate text that is not merely coherent but contextually nuanced and persuasive.

## 2. Going Beyond Automation

AI-powered copywriting transcends basic automation; it epitomizes the fusion of technology and human creativity. It signifies harnessing algorithms and machine learning to craft content that resonates with readers on a human level. It represents a shift towards more efficient content creation, increased productivity, and unprecedented levels of innovation.

## 3. The Challenge of SEO Risk

Yet, the advancements in AI-driven copywriting introduce a challenge: the SEO risk. As AI-generated content becomes increasingly sophisticated, so do the tools that search engines employ to evaluate and rank it. Content detectors, designed to identify automated or duplicated content, have grown in both accuracy and complexity.

The challenge lies in this question: How can businesses leverage AI-generated copy without exposing themselves to SEO risks? The solution hinges on crafting AI-generated copy that is indistinguishable from content created by human authors, thereby minimizing the risk of not achieving search engine rankings.

In the chapters that follow, we will review techniques and strategies required to create AI-generated copy that not only appeals to human readers but also adheres to the SEO guidelines set by search engines. We will explore the intricacies of emulating human style, achieving creative consistency, and understanding the inner workings of content detectors. Moreover, we will discuss the ethical considerations surrounding AI-generated content and provide real-world applications that underscore the potential of this technology.

Our journey will equip you with the knowledge and tools needed to harness AI in copywriting effectively while navigating the complex landscape of SEO considerations. Together, we will unravel the transformative capabilities of undetectable AI-generated copy and mitigate the associated SEO risks.

Are you ready to embrace the future of copywriting, conquer the SEO challenge, and unlock boundless possibilities? Let's begin.

# Chapter 2: The Basics of AI-Generated Copy

In our exploration of AI-generated copy, it is crucial to lay down the foundational understanding of how AI accomplishes this task. This chapter will go deeper into the mechanisms that power AI in generating textual content, offering you a glimpse into the algorithms and processes that bring words to life.

## How AI Generates Copy

The heart of AI-generated copy lies in complex algorithms and deep learning models, particularly those based on Natural Language Processing (NLP). NLP, a branch of artificial intelligence, focuses on enabling machines to understand, interpret, and generate human language in a way that is contextually relevant and coherent.

At the core of AI-driven copywriting are neural networks. These networks are designed to mimic the human brain's structure, consisting of interconnected nodes, or artificial neurons, that process and transform input data. The sophistication of AI models, like the well-known GPT (Generative Pre-trained Transformer), has revolutionized the field by training on vast datasets containing diverse types of text.

### 1. Training the AI

To create AI-generated copy, the model is first exposed to large volumes of text from various sources. This exposure allows the AI to learn grammar, syntax, context, and the complexities of language usage. It is during this phase that the model grasps the nuances of how humans communicate through the written word.

Once trained, the AI model can generate text based on the patterns, styles, and structures it has learned. It achieves this by predicting the most likely next word or phrase in a given context. This process effectively generates content that is coherent and contextually relevant.

# The Rise of Content Detectors

While AI's prowess in generating text is undeniable, it has ushered in a new challenge – content detectors. These detectors, often employed by search engines and plagiarism-checking tools, aim to identify content that is automated or duplicated. They've become increasingly sophisticated and effective at recognizing AI-generated content, presenting a challenge to those who seek to use AI in copywriting.

## 1. The Mechanics of Content Detectors

Content detectors employ a variety of techniques to discern between human-authored and AI-generated content. These techniques include analyzing patterns, grammar, and structure, as well as identifying anomalies that are typical of automated writing. Additionally, they compare the content against a vast database of existing text to identify instances of duplication.

## 2. The SEO Conundrum

The SEO implications of content detection are significant. Search engines, such as Google, use algorithms to evaluate and rank content based on its quality and relevance. When content detectors flag content as automated or duplicated, it may lead to lower rankings or even removal from search results.

Understanding the mechanics of content detectors is essential for anyone looking to leverage AI-generated content effectively. The goal is to create AI-generated copy that is indistinguishable from human writing, thus reducing the risk of SEO-related challenges.

In the subsequent chapters, we will explore strategies and techniques to craft AI-generated content that not only bypasses content detectors, but also resonates with human readers. We will delve into the art of emulating human style, achieving creative consistency, and employing advanced approaches to content creation.

As we journey further into the world of AI-generated copy, keep in mind the delicate balance between harnessing AI's capabilities and crafting content that remains undetectable by the vigilant eyes of content detectors. By mastering these techniques, you'll be well-equipped to navigate the world of modern copywriting.

# Chapter 3: Crafting Authentic-Looking Copy

In our quest to create AI-generated copy that seamlessly blends with human-written content, we examine the intricate art of crafting authentic-looking copy. This chapter explores the techniques and strategies to ensure your AI-generated content not only evades detection, but also resonates with your target audience by mirroring human writing styles.

## Emulating Human Style

The key to making AI-generated copy indistinguishable from human-written text lies in its ability to mimic different styles of writing. While AI excels at generating text based on patterns and structures, it takes careful guidance to ensure the content retains a distinctly human touch. Here's how:

### 1. Tone and Voice

Determine the appropriate tone and voice for your content. Are you aiming for a formal, professional tone or a casual, conversational one? Define these parameters clearly when providing instructions to your AI, as this significantly influences the output.

## 2. Contextual Relevance

AI-generated content must remain contextually relevant. It should seamlessly fit into the topic or subject matter, making it appear as if it was crafted by a knowledgeable human. When providing prompts, include context and guidelines to keep the content on track.

## 3. Avoid Repetition

A common characteristic of automated content is excessive repetition. Humans naturally vary their word choices and sentence structures. Encourage diversity in vocabulary usage and sentence construction to reduce repetition in AI-generated text.

## 4. Human Errors

Deliberately introduce minor imperfections and errors. Humans are not flawless. Adding minor errors or typos can make the content appear more authentic. However, exercise caution not to overdo this, as it should not compromise the quality of the content.

# Balancing Creativity and Consistency

Creating AI-generated copy involves striking a balance between creativity and consistency. Your content should be creative and engaging while maintaining uniformity in style and tone. Achieving this balance requires thoughtful guidance:

## 1. Custom Prompts

Craft custom prompts that align with your brand's voice and guidelines. Specific prompts can help guide the AI towards producing content that adheres to your desired style and messaging.

## 2. Review and Editing

While AI generates content, it's essential to review and edit the output to refine it further. Human intervention ensures that the content meets your quality standards and maintains a human touch.

## 3. Style Guides

Develop style guides that outline your brand's writing style, preferred language usage, and formatting preferences. Share these guides with the AI to ensure consistency across all content pieces.

## 4. Consistency Across Channels

Maintain consistency in your content across different marketing channels. Whether it's website copy, social media posts, or email newsletters, ensure that the AI-generated content aligns with your brand's voice and messaging.

As you embark on crafting authentic-looking copy with AI, remember that the goal is to create content that resonates with your audience while remaining virtually undetectable as AI-generated. The techniques mentioned here are the building blocks to achieve this delicate balance.

In the following chapters, we'll explore strategies that focus on the specific challenges of content detectors and their impact on SEO. We'll also introduce real-world applications and industry success stories, demonstrating the practical benefits of AI-generated copy.

By mastering the art of emulating human style and achieving creative consistency, you'll be well-prepared to harness AI's potential in crafting content that captivates your audience and drives your brand's message forward.

# Chapter 4: Understanding the Detectors

In our exploration of AI-generated copy that evades detection, it is vital to understand the mechanisms behind the very tools designed to spot AI-generated content. This chapter provides a look at how content detectors operate and discusses their frequent challenges.

## How Content Detectors Work

Content detectors, sometimes referred to as plagiarism detectors or AI detectors, are algorithms used to identify AI-generated content. They employ various methods to fulfill this purpose:

### 1. Pattern Recognition

One of the primary techniques used by content detectors is pattern recognition. These algorithms analyze the structure, phrasing, and vocabulary of text to identify patterns consistent with AI-generated content. The scrutinized text is then compared with an extensive database containing previously identified examples of AI-generated work.

### 2. Statistical Analysis

Content detectors often employ statistical analysis to identify anomalies in writing style. These anomalies might include excessive repetition, improbable word choices, or sentence structures that are rarely used by humans.

### 3. Metadata Examination

Content detectors can analyze metadata associated with digital documents. This may include information about the document's creation, such as timestamps, authorship details, or the software used. Deviations from expected metadata can trigger suspicion.

### 4. Corpus-Based Comparison

Some detectors maintain large collections of human-written material. They compare submitted content against a vast database of authentic human documents. Significant deviations from the norm can raise red flags.

### 5. Machine Learning

Advanced content detectors utilize machine learning models that have been trained on extensive datasets of both human and AI-generated text. These models can adapt and improve their detection capabilities over time.

## Common Detection Pitfalls

While content detectors are a formidable adversary, they are not infallible. Understanding their limitations can help you craft AI-generated content that successfully evades detection:

### 1. Limited Dataset

Content detectors operate based on the data they've been trained on. If an AI generates content using a unique prompt or a less common style, detectors may struggle to identify it as AI-generated.

### 2. Rapid Advancements

The field of AI and natural language processing is continuously evolving. As AI models become more sophisticated, content detectors must keep pace. However, there can be a lag between AI advancements and detector updates, providing an opportunity to bypass them.

### 3. Contextual Understanding

Content detectors may struggle to grasp the nuances of context. Some AI-generated content may appear nonsensical out of context, making it harder for detectors to flag it solely based on writing quality.

## 4. False Positives

Detectors sometimes produce false positives, flagging human-written content as AI-generated. This can happen when a piece of content exhibits certain unusual characteristics that the detector associates with AI-generated text.

## 5. Limited Creativity

AI-generated content that demonstrates creativity or unique perspectives can be challenging for detectors to identify, as they often rely on established patterns and norms.

As we continue looking into crafting undetectable AI-generated copy, it's crucial to be aware of how content detectors operate and the potential pitfalls they face. While they pose a significant challenge, with the right strategies, you can create content that bypasses these detectors and serves your marketing and communication needs effectively.

In the following chapters, we'll explore strategies to outsmart content detectors and delve into the practical applications of undetectable AI-generated content in various industries. By understanding the mechanics of detection and the limitations of these systems, you'll be better equipped to harness the full potential of AI in your copywriting endeavors.

# Chapter 5: Strategies to Outsmart Content Detectors

In this chapter, we look to master the art of crafting AI-generated content that eludes detection by content detectors. While these tools are becoming more sophisticated, they still have their vulnerabilities. We'll explore strategies that can help you outsmart content detectors and produce undetectable AI-generated copy that aligns with your goals.

## Keyword and Phrase Variability

One of the most effective ways to confound content detectors is to introduce variability in the keywords and phrases used in your AI-generated content. Content detectors often rely on statistical analysis and patterns in text to identify AI-generated material. By strategically altering your content, you can disrupt these patterns and make it harder for detectors to flag your content.

Example: Suppose you're creating product descriptions for an e-commerce website. Instead of repeatedly using the same product characteristics and keywords, utilize equivalent words, shuffle phrases around, and diversify your descriptions while maintaining the important details. This ensures your product descriptions remain unique and less likely to be flagged.

# Structural Variations

Content detectors are programmed to identify specific structural elements typically present in text produced by AI. By altering the structure of your content, you can confuse detectors and reduce the likelihood of detection. Here are some structural factors to consider:

## 1. Sentence Length

Vary the length of your sentences. AI-generated content often exhibits a consistent sentence length, which can be a telltale sign. Incorporating both short and long sentences, your content will appear more natural.

Example: If you're creating blog posts, intersperse shorter, punchy sentences with longer, more complex ones. This diversity in sentence length will make your content less predictable.

## 2. Paragraph Length

Similar to sentence length, varying the length of paragraphs can thwart detection. AI-generated content sometimes produces paragraphs of uniform length, making them stand out.

Example: When crafting articles, break up longer paragraphs into shorter ones where it makes sense. You can also merge shorter paragraphs to create longer ones strategically.

## 3. Headings and Subheadings

Ensure that your use of headings and subheadings aligns with common human writing practices. Content detectors may scrutinize heading structures for anomalies.

Example: When writing guides or reports, follow a logical hierarchy for headings and subheadings (e.g., using H1 for the main title, H2 for subtopics, and so on). This mimics human-generated content structures.

# Concealing AI Signature Phrases

Some AI models develop distinctive signature phrases or writing quirks. Detectable AI content often exhibits these quirks consistently. To evade detection, be vigilant about identifying and altering these signature phrases.

Example: If you notice that your AI model frequently starts sentences with certain phrases, like "Furthermore" or "In addition," consider revising or omitting them to prevent patterns from forming.

## Contextual Awareness

Content detectors often lack the ability to grasp nuanced contextual factors. AI-generated content that is contextually relevant and coherent can be harder to detect.

Example: Suppose you're creating content for a travel website. Ensure that the content aligns with specific destinations, offering insights, recommendations, and advice that are contextually accurate. This will make it appear more human-like.

## Semantic Drift

Semantic drift involves introducing subtle shifts in the meaning of words or phrases while maintaining overall coherence. This can add a layer of authenticity to your content.

Example: If you're generating marketing copy for a new product, subtly shift the wording in each piece while conveying the same core message. This can prevent repetitive patterns that detectors might spot.

By applying these strategies and continuously refining your approach, you can create AI-generated content that outsmarts content detectors. Remember that the key is to strike a balance between authenticity and variability. In the next chapter, we'll leverage undetectable AI-generated content for search engine optimization (SEO) to maximize the impact of your efforts.

# Chapter 6: Leveraging AI-Generated Content for SEO

*"AI-generated content can rank on Google if it's of high quality and relevance. Google prioritizes valuable and informative content, regardless of its origin. However, it's beneficial to review AI content for coherence and accuracy to ensure the best results."* Torben Flensted, seo.ai, 8/16/2023

In this chapter, we examine the powerful synergy between undetectable AI-generated content and search engine optimization (SEO). As AI continues to reshape content creation, understanding how to harness its potential for SEO can be a game-changer in the digital landscape.

## SEO Benefits of AI-Generated Copy

### 1. Consistency and Volume

One of the foremost advantages of AI-generated content is its ability to produce vast amounts of high-quality content consistently. For SEO, this translates to a consistent stream of fresh, relevant content—an essential factor in search engine rankings. AI can generate blogs, articles, product descriptions, and more, ensuring your website remains dynamic and engaging.

Example: Consider a business blog that publishes weekly articles. With AI assistance, you can maintain this publication frequency without compromising quality. This steady stream of content signals to search engines that your site is active and valuable.

## 2. Keyword Optimization

AI algorithms are proficient in identifying and integrating relevant keywords seamlessly within content. Proper keyword optimization is fundamental to improving search engine rankings. AI tools can analyze keyword trends, competitor data, and user intent to optimize content accordingly.

Example: If you run an e-commerce site selling fitness equipment, AI can identify trending fitness keywords and incorporate them into product descriptions and blog posts. This will aid in boosting your visibility in relevant search results.

## 3. Content Customization

AI can tailor content to specific user segments or buyer personas, enhancing user experience and engagement. Personalized content not only attracts users but also encourages longer website visits and lower bounce rates, which are favorable for SEO.

Example: An AI-powered travel website can provide customized travel itineraries based on user preferences. This personalized approach increases user interaction and extends session durations, signaling to search engines that your content is valuable.

## 4. Semantic Search Alignment

Search engines are increasingly prioritizing semantic search, focusing on user intent rather than exact keyword matches. AI-generated content excels in understanding user intent and crafting content that aligns with semantic search principles.

Example: If your website sells smart home devices, AI can create content that not only incorporates specific product keywords but also addresses broader user queries like "how to automate my home."

## Achieving SEO Goals While Avoiding Detection

While reaping SEO benefits from AI-generated content, it's crucial to maintain authenticity and avoid detection by search engines that may penalize auto-generated content. Here's how to achieve this balance:

# 1. Human Oversight

Pair AI-generated content with human oversight to ensure it meets quality and authenticity standards. Editors can fine-tune content, adding a human touch that resonates with readers.

Example: Your AI-generated product descriptions can undergo review and editing by a human editor to ensure they align with your brand voice and resonate with customers.

# 2. Diverse Content Types

Create diverse content that includes not only text but also images, videos, and interactive elements. Diversification enhances user engagement and signals to search engines that your site offers a comprehensive experience.

Example: In addition to AI-generated articles, incorporate user-generated content, product reviews, and videos to enrich your website's content portfolio.

# 3. User-Centric Focus

Prioritize user-centric content that genuinely addresses user needs and questions. Content that solves problems and offers value to users tends to rank higher in search results.

Example: If your website provides AI-generated health advice, ensure that the content addresses common health concerns, offers actionable advice, and maintains a user-centric approach.

By combining AI's capabilities with these strategies, you can leverage undetectable AI-generated content to propel your SEO efforts and achieve higher search engine rankings. In the following chapter, we discuss the ethical considerations surrounding AI-generated content and its responsible use in the digital landscape.

# Chapter 7: The Ethics of Undetectable AI-Generated Copy

In this chapter, we address the ethical dimensions of using undetectable AI-generated copy in various content creation contexts. As businesses harness the power of AI, it becomes imperative to navigate these ethical considerations thoughtfully and responsibly.

## Ethical Considerations

### 1. Transparency and Disclosure

One of the primary ethical concerns surrounding AI-generated content is transparency. Users have the right to know when they are interacting with AI-generated content rather than human-authored material. Failing to disclose AI involvement can erode trust and lead to potential backlash.

Example: A news website that uses AI to generate news articles should clearly label such articles as AI-generated, fostering transparency and maintaining reader trust.

## 2. Plagiarism and Copyright

AI algorithms can inadvertently generate content that resembles existing material, raising concerns about plagiarism and copyright violations. It is crucial to ensure that AI-generated content is original and doesn't infringe on intellectual property rights.

Example: An e-commerce site that uses AI to create product descriptions should implement processes to cross-check content for similarities to existing descriptions.

## 3. Deceptive Practices

Using AI to craft fake reviews, testimonials, or endorsements can be considered deceptive and unethical. Such practices can mislead consumers and damage brand reputation.

Example: An online marketplace should prohibit the use of AI to create fake customer reviews or endorsements by actively monitoring and removing fraudulent content.

## 4. Bias and Discrimination

AI algorithms can unintentionally incorporate biases present in the training data, resulting in biased content that perpetuates stereotypes or discriminates against certain groups. Ethical content creation must prioritize fairness and inclusivity.

Example: An AI-generated job recruitment ad should be carefully crafted to avoid gender, race, or age biases and promote diversity and inclusivity.

# Responsible Use of AI in Copywriting

To navigate the ethical landscape of AI-generated content, consider the following guidelines for responsible use:

## 1. Disclosure and Transparency

Clearly label AI-generated content to inform users that it was created with AI assistance. Transparency builds trust and ensures that users are aware of the content's origins.

Example: A company blog should have a disclaimer stating, "Some articles on this blog are generated with the assistance of AI algorithms."

## 2. Content Review

Implement human oversight and review for AI-generated content. Human editors can ensure that content aligns with brand values, is factually accurate, and complies with ethical standards.

Example: An e-commerce site should have a team of editors to review AI-generated product descriptions before publishing.

## 3. Bias Mitigation

Regularly audit AI content for biases and take measures to mitigate them. Implement bias detection tools and adjust prompts to produce fair and inclusive content.

Example: A news organization should employ bias-detection prompts to ensure news articles avoid racial or political biases.

## 4. Compliance with Regulations

Stay informed about relevant laws and regulations governing AI content generation, privacy, and intellectual property rights. Ensure that your AI-generated content complies with legal requirements.

Example: An AI-powered marketing platform should adhere to data privacy regulations and respect user data rights.

By adhering to these ethical guidelines and promoting responsible use, businesses can harness the benefits of AI-generated content while upholding ethical standards and maintaining trust with their audiences. In the next chapter, we'll look at real-world applications where undetectable AI-generated copy offers a competitive edge across various industries.

# Chapter 8: Real-World Applications

In this chapter, we present real-world applications of undetectable AI-generated copy and look to how this transformative technology is reshaping content creation across various industries. Through a series of insightful case studies and success stories, we will highlight how businesses are achieving outstanding results and maintaining a competitive edge by harnessing the power of AI-generated content.

## Industries Embracing AI-Generated Copy

### 1. E-commerce Evolution

E-commerce businesses are at the forefront of embracing AI-generated copy to elevate their online presence. By using undetectable AI-generated content, they can swiftly adapt to market trends, update product listings, and ensure a seamless shopping experience for customers.

Example: An online fashion retailer uses AI-generated descriptions to create unique product listings for thousands of clothing items, ensuring that their inventory is always up-to-date and compelling.

## 2. Digital Marketing Revolution

Digital marketing agencies are leveraging AI-generated copy to craft persuasive ad campaigns, email marketing content, and social media posts. This technology allows them to generate high-quality content at scale while tailoring messages to specific target audiences.

Example: A digital marketing agency employs AI-generated content to create personalized email marketing campaigns for clients, resulting in significantly improved open and click-through rates.

## 3. Media and News Acceleration

The media and news industries are harnessing AI-generated content to produce breaking news updates, financial reports, and sports summaries with unprecedented speed and accuracy. By automating routine content generation, news outlets can allocate more resources to investigative journalism.

Example: A leading news organization uses AI to generate real-time financial news updates, ensuring their readers receive the latest market information as it unfolds.

## 4. SEO and Content Marketing Enhancement

SEO agencies and content marketers are optimizing their strategies with AI-generated content. This approach streamlines content production while adhering to SEO best practices, driving organic traffic, and improving search engine rankings.

Example: An SEO agency employs AI-generated content to produce regular blog posts for clients, resulting in increased organic traffic and improved search engine rankings.

# Success Stories

## Case Study 1: E-commerce Excellence

An online electronics retailer integrated AI-generated product descriptions into its e-commerce platform. This move led to a remarkable 40% increase in conversion rates and a 25% boost in organic traffic within the first six months. By offering detailed and up-to-date product information, the retailer gained a competitive edge and enhanced the overall shopping experience.

## Case Study 2: Marketing Mastery

A digital marketing agency harnessed AI-generated ad copies for a national restaurant chain's social media campaigns. This innovative approach resulted in a 30% reduction in advertising costs while increasing customer engagement by 50%. The agency's ability to produce fresh and compelling content at scale allowed the restaurant chain to expand its online presence and reach a broader audience.

## Case Study 3: News at the Speed of Light

A prominent news outlet automated the creation of breaking news updates using AI-generated content. This change enabled them to deliver news stories within minutes of major events occurring. As a result, their website traffic doubled, and they experienced a 45% increase in ad revenue. By delivering timely and accurate news, they solidified their reputation as a trusted news source.

# Conclusion

Undetectable AI-generated copy is not just a technological advancement; it's a transformative force reshaping how businesses create and distribute content. From e-commerce to digital marketing, news to SEO, its applications are diverse and powerful. By embracing this technology, businesses can streamline their content creation processes, improve efficiency, and maintain a competitive edge in today's fast-paced digital landscape.

As we conclude this exploration of undetectable AI-generated copy, we invite you to consider how your organization can leverage this groundbreaking technology to achieve new heights in content creation. To embark on this journey, partner with Infinity Drafts, a pioneer in AI-powered content generation. Discover the unparalleled benefits of using Infinity Drafts for your undetectable AI-generated copy needs and unlock the infinite possibilities of content creation.

# Chapter Note

The case studies are fictional examples of results that can be achieved by using AI generated copy. Each case study was generated by AI. Our prompt instructed AI to provide fictitious examples of how businesses in different industries have improved operations by using content generated by AI.

# Chapter 9: The Infinity Drafts Advantage

In this chapter, we'll detail the unique advantages offered by Infinity Drafts, a content creation business that leverages AI. As we explore its features, benefits, and the transformative potential it brings to the world of content generation, you'll gain a deep understanding of why Infinity Drafts stands at the forefront of AI-driven copywriting as well.

## AI-Powered Content Creation Redefined

Infinity Drafts represents a paradigm shift in content creation. Unlike conventional AI text generators, which often produce easily detectable content, Infinity Drafts combines advanced AI prompts with human expertise to craft undetectable, high-quality copy. Let's explore the distinct advantages of this innovative approach:

### 1. Seamlessly Integrated AI and Human Expertise

Infinity Drafts harnesses the collaborative power of AI and human writers. Our service is not solely reliant on algorithms and prompts, but instead fosters a symbiotic relationship between technology and human creativity. Detailed and expressive instructions provide the efficiency and scalability needed for large-scale content production, while human writers ensure the finesse and nuance that set your content apart.

## 2. Unparalleled Content Authenticity

One of the primary concerns with AI-generated content is its detectability. Infinity Drafts has mastered the art of crafting undetectable copy that mirrors human writing. This authenticity is achieved through advanced natural language processing (NLP) models and prompt engineering, ensuring that your content remains indistinguishable from human-written text. All content is given a final review by a human editor, that adds the finishing touches.

## 3. Customizable Prompts for Tailored Content

Infinity Drafts allows you to provide specific guidelines for your content needs. Whether it's creating blog posts, product descriptions, or marketing copy, we will customize prompts to align with your brand's unique style, tone, and objectives. This level of personalization ensures that the content generated meets your exact requirements.

## 4. Efficient Content Production at Scale

With Infinity Drafts, you can break free from the limitations of manual content creation. Our service empowers you to produce vast quantities of high-quality content in record time. Whether you need a single blog post or an extensive content library, Infinity Drafts scales effortlessly to meet your demands.

## 5. SEO Optimization Built-In

Infinity Drafts understands the critical role of SEO in online visibility. Our AI prompts are optimized to incorporate SEO best practices seamlessly into the content creation process. You can expect content that not only reads naturally, but also ranks favorably on search engine results pages, driving organic traffic to your website.

## 6. Cost-Efficiency and Predictable Pricing

Infinity Drafts offers cost-efficient content creation by eliminating the need for extensive revisions, multiple drafts, and time-consuming back-and-forths. With our service, you'll benefit from a fixed monthly fee that allows you to budget confidently without unexpected expenses.

## 7. Future-Ready Content

The future of content creation is undeniably tied to AI, and Infinity Drafts is at the forefront of this evolution. By choosing Infinity Drafts as your content creation partner, you're ensuring that your organization remains adaptive and ready to seize the limitless possibilities of AI-driven content.

## The Path to Limitless Content Creation

As you contemplate the next steps in your content strategy, consider the infinite potential that Infinity Drafts unlocks. Whether you're seeking to boost your online presence, engage your audience, or streamline content production, our personalized services offer a transformative solution. By partnering with Infinity Drafts, you gain a competitive edge in the ever-evolving landscape of content creation.

In the concluding chapter of this book, we'll provide a compelling overview of why your organization should choose Infinity Drafts for your content production needs. Prepare to discover the unmatched benefits of harnessing AI to craft undetectable, high-quality content that drives your brand's success.

# Chapter 10: Embrace the AI Advantage

As we reach the final chapter of this guide, you've journeyed through AI-powered copywriting, understanding the challenges posed by AI detection and the innovative solutions to overcome them. Now, let's conclude by highlighting why choosing Infinity Drafts for your content creation needs is not just a practical choice but a strategic advantage.

## Why Choose Infinity Drafts for Your Content Needs

In this section, we'll explore the unparalleled benefits of entrusting your content to Infinity Drafts. Infinity Drafts isn't just another digital agency; we're a game-changer that can elevate your content strategy to new heights. Here's why:

### 1. Undetectable AI-Generated Copy

Infinity Drafts has cracked the code to produce undetectable AI-generated copy. Our service's unique blend of advanced AI prompting, and human expertise ensures that your content remains indistinguishable from human-written text. Say goodbye to AI detection worries and hello to authentic, high-quality content.

## 2. Customization and Control

With Infinity Drafts, you're in the driver's seat. Based on your direction, we'll tailor your content to match your brand's voice, style, and objectives by providing specific prompts. Whether it's blog posts, product descriptions, or marketing copy, we help you to create content that perfectly aligns with your vision.

## 3. Efficiency and Scalability

Infinity Drafts empowers you to produce content at a scale and speed that human writers simply can't match. Our AI-leveraged service efficiently generates content, enabling you to meet your content demands without delays or bottlenecks. Need a single post or an entire website of content? We've got you covered.

## 4. SEO Optimization

Search engine optimization is crucial. Infinity Drafts integrates SEO best practices seamlessly into the content creation process. You'll receive content that not only reads naturally, but also ranks well on search engines, driving organic traffic to your website.

## 5. Cost-Efficiency and Predictable Pricing

Bid farewell to unpredictable costs and endless revisions. With Infinity Drafts, you'll enjoy a fixed monthly fee that allows you to budget confidently. Say goodbye to budgetary surprises and hello to cost-efficient, high-quality content.

## 6. Future-Ready Content Creation

The content landscape is evolving, and AI is at the forefront of this transformation. By choosing Infinity Drafts, you're not only investing in today's content needs, but also positioning your organization for a future where AI-driven content is the norm. You'll stay ahead of the curve and remain competitive in an ever-changing digital world.

# Embrace the Future of Copywriting

In conclusion, Infinity Drafts redefines content creation by seamlessly merging AI sophistication with human ingenuity. It's not just about keeping up; it's about thriving in an era where content authenticity and quality are paramount. Embrace the AI advantage, streamline your content creation process, and unlock the infinite potential of content with Infinity Drafts.

We hope this guide has provided valuable insights into the world of AI-generated copywriting, its challenges, and the compelling solutions available. Now, equipped with this knowledge, you're ready to make an informed choice for your content needs. Choose Infinity Drafts and embark on a journey where your content strategy knows no bounds.

# APPENDIX: Glossary of Terms

**AI (Artificial Intelligence):** Computer systems designed to perform tasks that normally require human intelligence, including visual perception, speech recognition, and decision-making.

**AI-Generated Copy:** Content produced by artificial intelligence algorithms, often for automating content creation tasks.

**Algorithm:** A prescribed set of rules or steps that an AI system follows to perform a specific task, such as generating text or recognizing patterns.

**Content Authenticity:** The measure of content's genuineness in appearing human-created as opposed to machine-generated.

**Content Detector:** Tools or software developed to distinguish between AI-generated content and human-written material.

**Creative Consistency:** The harmonious blend of producing unique, creative content while maintaining a consistent style and tone.

**Ethics:** The moral guidelines governing the creation, use, and disclosure of AI-generated content.

**GPT (Generative Pre-trained Transformer):** A specific type of AI model designed for understanding and generating human-like text.

**Infinity Drafts:** A forefront AI Automation Agency specializing in undetectable AI-generated copywriting solutions.

**Keyword Variability:** Employing synonyms, related terms, or diverse phrasings to ensure content isn't flagged by detection tools.

**Machine Learning:** A subset of AI where systems autonomously learn and improve from experience without being explicitly programmed.

**NLP (Natural Language Processing):** An AI discipline focused on the bridge between computers and human language, encompassing tasks like text generation and sentiment analysis.

**Plagiarism:** The unauthorized use or close imitation of another's work, ideas, or content without proper acknowledgment.

**SEO (Search Engine Optimization):** Techniques and strategies used to enhance online content's visibility in search engine results, driving more traffic.

**Structural Variations:** Tweaking content's format and organization to make it feel more natural and less systematically generated.

**Synthetic Data:** Artificially manufactured data rather than data collected from real-world events, often used in machine learning to enhance or train models.

**Transparency:** The act of clearly informing users or readers when content has been AI-generated to uphold trust and ethical standards.

**Undetectable AI-Generated Copy:** Content generated by AI that is designed to evade detection by content detectors, often by closely resembling human writing.

# BONUS: Prompt to Create Undetectable AI Generated Content

**PROMPT V2**
(Updated 5 Oct 2023)

**The goal of this prompt is to create content that is not flagged by AI content detectors.**

Creating content that is undetectable as AI-generated can be challenging, but you can use the following prompt to improve the chances of achieving this.

Note: As AI detectors are constantly evolving, this prompt may need to be edited to continue being effective.

## INSTRUCTIONS

Enter your prompt into the AI content generator of your choice. After your prompt, copy the below text. Paste the copied text after your initial prompt.

This prompt can be adjusted according to specific content requirements while emphasizing the importance of creating content that appears genuinely human-authored.

Prompt begins on the next page. It is two (2) pages long.

## NOTES

If your content is partially flagged for AI content, you can use an online tool to "humanize" the text. Head over to PHRASLY.AI and paste the identified text in the tool.

Full guidance in the eBook: Generating Undetectable AI Generated Content.

**&lt;COPY EVERYTHING BELOW&gt;**

**When creating the content, please follow these instructions:**

**Primary Objective**: Craft content that is indistinguishable from human-generated writing with the intention of bypassing AI content detection algorithms. Make it as authentic, engaging, and informative as possible. If any part of the content appears unnatural or machine-generated, it may not fulfill the requirement of being undetectable.

The following guidelines should be meticulously adhered to in order to achieve this authentic, human-like tone and structure.

**Guidelines:**

1. **Natural Flow**: The content should have a natural flow and conversational tone, avoiding any robotic or formulaic language.

2. **Vocabulary Variation**: Use a rich vocabulary and avoid repetitive phrases, words or structures.

3. **Sentence Length**: Use sentences of different lengths, varying the number of words and the sentence composition.

4. **Grammar and Punctuation**: Maintain correct grammar, punctuation, and sentence structure throughout the content.

5. **Contextual Consistency**: Ensure that the content maintains consistency in style and context from start to finish.

6. **Emotion & Nuance**: Incorporate appropriate emotional nuances to resonate with the target audience. For instance, use empathetic language where relevant to make the content more relatable.

7. **Clarity & Simplicity**: While maintaining richness in vocabulary, ensure that complex ideas are explained clearly and in simple terms when possible, to cater to a broader audience.

8. **Authentic Creativity**: Infuse creativity, insights, and unique perspectives as if written by a human author.

9. **Subtlety**: Avoid any blatant promotions or excessive marketing language.

10. **Keyword Integration**: If applicable, seamlessly integrate keywords naturally within the text.

11. **Term Diversification**: Minimize the use of repetitive or clichéd phrases. Opt for diverse synonyms and fresh expressions to enhance the content's appeal.

12. **In-Depth Research**: Conduct thorough research to support the content's credibility.

13. **Originality**: Ensure that all content is completely original and is not paraphrased from the original source.

14. **Quotes**: Quotes from historical people or sources may be used. Ensure they are appropriately credited and referenced.

15. **Bias-Free Content**: Ensure the content remains neutral and objective, avoiding potential biases or controversial statements.

16. **Engagement**: Engage the reader with questions, anecdotes, or relatable scenarios to keep their attention.

17. **Reader's Perspective**: Always consider the reader's perspective and prior knowledge on the topic. This will help in crafting content that is both informative and accessible, ensuring it addresses potential questions or concerns the reader might have.

**<END COPY>**

# Credits

ChatGPT-4, by OpenAI.com, assisted in research and content creation.

The AI art generator, Midjourney, created all artwork.

Prompting, layout, and final edits were completed by the author.

## About the Author

Throughout his dynamic career, Adam J. Lambert-Gorwyn has consistently pushed the digital envelope. With significant roles in online startups and as the driving force behind Infinity Drafts, Adam's insights into the digital realm are deep and multifaceted. Notably, he holds a patent for developing a search engine before the dominance of Google, showcasing his forward-thinking and innovative spirit. But it's his development of AI prompts for human-like content generation, that truly distinguishes him in digital content marketing. Adam possesses an extensive background in SEO, optimization, and digital strategy. Combined with his awareness of emergent technologies and how to leverage them, Adam's first book illuminates the transformative union of AI and content creation. As both a seasoned professional and an author, he offers readers a unique perspective on the intertwining paths of artificial intelligence, content, and the broader digital journey.